MW00423242

JUSTICE

Justice

by Tomaž Šalamun
translated by Michael Thomas Taren

Black Ocean
Boston · Detroit · Chicago

Black Ocean
P.O. Box 52030
Boston, MA 02205
blackocean.org

Cover Art and Design by Abby Haddican | abbyhaddican.com
Book Design by Nikkita Cohoon | nikkita.co

ISBN 978-1-939568-11-3

Library of Congress Cataloging-in-Publication Data

Šalamun, Tomaž.
  [Poems. Selections. English]
  Justice / Tomaž Šalamun ; translated by Michael Thomas Taren.
—First edition.
      pages cm
  "Translated from Slovenian to English, Justice is a selection
of previously untranslated poetry of Tomaž Šalamun that spans
several collections and unpublished works from his career"
--Publisher's note.
  ISBN 978-1-939568-11-3
  1. Šalamun, Tomaž--Translations into English. I. Taren, Michael
Thomas, translator. II. Title.
  PG1919.29.A5A6 2015
  891.8'415--dc23
                                                  2015030419

FIRST EDITION

CONTENTS

THE WATERFALL

I VALUE MY SEMEN

JUSTICE

RED MUSTANG

THE NIGHTINGALE

WINDY BUT NICE

THE
WATERFALL

Not a minute of my life
was lost.
Tanks were there
and altars in paper boxes.
White grass burned in white flames
and I was on cocaine.

There are pithy grapes.
I stay pinned.
It rains.
It rains from your fingers.
We both rose.
We both met.
We both stopped.
I will flutter.
I will flutter another time.
Your knuckles crack.
I have hair.
I saw night.
I was close.
I was there.
You have azure rooms.
There are cars.
I'm heedless.
Stop me.
I stay pinned.
I divided me and you from me and you.
I had wings.
It was heard of.
They covered me with a carpet.
I heard drops.

I swam.
With my head I touched the page.
The sea rose.
The bridge is walked through.
There are no doormen.

A SNUFF MOTH

I was born like a snuff moth.
The nail went barely below my neck.
When I was fourteen
I read Ivo Andrić,
how the Turks tortured Christians,
they impaled them
so by dawn they've seen the pole
coming out of their wound and they died.
Fates pitied my face,
on a piece of paper they had written
for me the story of oysters.
I went to Istria, to the deep bay.
I dived and put oysters
on the nail below my neck.
I had dived three times,
the nail melted,
I poured nectar into my scar,
and threw the sheet of paper into the sea.
The last blow to the sheet of paper was
that the Algerian marine exploded it.
When I was twenty-nine years old
I watched a fuck film in New York,
how they shoved into his rectum a long
fake dick of a handsome guy who looked

exactly like my friend in Yugoslavia.
They turned it round and pushed it like a drill
until it came out through his mouth.
He looked happy, then he said
"pretty wiped out." I was totally afraid
for him and had written him a letter,
the story about the oysters.
He went to Istria, to the deep bay.
He dived and lit his bowels with oysters.
He had dived three times,
the film reel disappeared.
He watered outer walls of his skin with nectar,
and threw the letter into the sea.
The last blow to the letter was
that a yogi who practiced near
Neretva River's delta swallowed it.

HER DREAMS FOR HER BIRTHDAY

All at once I was in Russia. I don't know
with whom, with Travitza or with Harriet,
we roared with laughter. In Russia, I stepped
directly from my apartment which had
streets and giant rooms. There were soldiers
everywhere. The meat hanged from the
shack. So they do have meat we said to
ourselves, but it turned out the meat was only
for the canteen. We passed them. A certain
woman came running, she told us her son
in Moscow filed a request and we should
see if the request was being processed.
We promised to do that and proceeded
through the woods roaring with laughter.

Hannes drew the shoe and the duck,
Tamsin drew the lady with the chalk.

I, five years old, have made
a book of poems for my mom's birthday,
now owned by Nina Souvan who
doesn't want to give it back.

humor is not for the chosen
dear guardian angel mine, protect my mom and dad
my nonna and nonno, my granny and grandfather
aunt ines and uncle bojan
and my brother let him be born healthy
clubs, a punch, pan american, the tibetan book of the dead
the youngest salesman, lice
father! father! near water! leant by water!
shrieks, upanishads, a toboggan and lamps
here he skated, licked a salty dandelion
it was scratched, sketches lined with wings
a huge vacuum cleaner, a filter like drying hoods
a home expanded by a simulator, warm wine
an elephant's head, torturings, nailed bones & UDBA men
a zoo, my uncle plays with *fondue*
he throws his tits on the poster, swedenborg is a skunk
with shrimps, big ships my stock, butter
teddy bear! teddy bear! with whip, the dreadful dreams
a black lacquer, a black soul
white teeth, black štefka with her big white ass
in vikrče! where you peed in your pants, man
o emotions!
where angels gathered on the tops of spruce firs
where in bohinj waves are taller than grown-ups

scout songs, our granny is slapped by katka
you sweat old whore guermantes
the grease! rab! the conflagration!

HORN

As topos of Spaniards:
in gold and in flintstone, Andalusia.

Angels spring in the air,
topos of circling surfaces.

Immeasurable blurs,
bombarding surfaces of the surface,

the tent above three beams
of three surface's angles:

destroy the dwelling.

DON

Cornelius will come into my poems.
He wants to come.
Cornelius will eat and dismantle me,
eat and dismantle me,
and will roar with laughter, brightly tossing me away.

Don stares at me across the table.
His gaze is discreet.

Don removes the flowers and says that I'm his
mentor.

YOUR SISTER

The death certificate had an unusual scent.
It smelled of a dirty duck.

Still more, it smelled of stones,
of pearls lying on the dirty duck's

toes. The reins also smelled.
And the horse's tooth.

The death certificate had a mother,
a father, a grandmother

and a duck. Robbers marched in along
City Hall. I applauded, I applauded,

lying on my belly, watching trains
with a gentle plant in my

mouth. The sky was soldered.
The frogspawn burned in the fireplace.

GOLD-GREEN DROPS OF LIGHT

I feel as if I all my life
lied naked on

the rocks, me, the sun child.
I was a windlass.

The lord of bread and semen.
Mountain ridges kept

collapsing. It flashed in the stones.
I ran behind the steely wire,

gave everything. I'm a sidewalk.
The milt confused me. Now

Michael is here. Toofa. A giant
piece of meat in the cliffs

among Somalis. The ostrich is my
brother. Hidden.

ZEUS AND HERA

Tendrils in antiquity had
a symbolic meaning.
They were pieces of Zeus's beard.
Poseidon had to nail his footstool
by himself. He cracked jokes and called
names and then jumped below
the typical surface of the Ionian sea,
to rob amphorae foundered by Phoenicians.
Hera bit the table with her legs
and in pure rage passed a decree:
Nationalize the Mediterranean basin!
Boxes of gold just jumped on
olive branches. A mohair red sweater
fluttered from Olympus to
the Athenian sauna.
But Poseidon pushed water to the stairs,
stepped on a chopping block
and with a whip lacerated the tripe of
fat decadents who day and night
sucked tender boys' penises.
Their thighs inflamed.
Sawdust flitted from their mouth.
Between the dot and the dot of sawdust
he once again hanged tendrils,
to gain them a symbolic meaning.

SYMBOLIC ORDER

My Lord, provide me with a little neck and breasts.
Storks hang on my shoulders and teeth. I eat

from my throat. Northern Lights are possible.
A pink vase. Wet and knitted chairs. What if

there was a cotton under a little plaque and the young
mister catfish killed? Who would loot scents

for my mill stones and interview *maman* with curls?
If they would place my puppets on the back

of a camel, it'd do for me too. The camel still wore
bites from the grizzly's teeth, one puppet's

finger broke into blood. Should I wrap and pamper
it? Maybe I could cut it off with a lego cube.

Enough that Aladdin and a gray donkey carry water
far, far from Jerusalem as in Christ times.

THE HOUR

Greasy pearls, the welded out birds,
why? why?
I live.
St. John the Baptist,
the pear falls, the child grows up.
I rush to my job, Bronzino, the same as you
who painted him with the fur coat and
as the stained.
Seven faces, seven mouths.
The precipice between toes,
as the enraptured.
The called-up, the apprehensive, the naked,
the taut as a string, do you crawl water
or do you leave it to flow?
Do you give drops in the form of a surface?
The skin blackens. The skin was white.
You're in front of a big, horrible gesture
toward the expanse, in front
of the face and body of the Son.

FATHER POURS TEETH

Wild boars anoint me.
They tear off

my head. I stand
in the factory's

garret. Incas caress
moms. I'm a

Merovingian. The fish
Goldy. My soul

is a tiny bottle, shot off
with paper

spitballs by an
Aztec, so

he can oil himself
with its contents.

The girl in Turkey lies down on the rocks,
her fiancé takes a picture of her.
Her body boils,
rocks threaten her.
She knows the photo will be taken.
Rocks crumble.
She knows the sun shines.
The fiancé watches the photo
and thinks about that summer.
A rage seizes him.

PEUGEOT

He saw a lamp on Peugeot,
he smashed it.

The same morning he
cut himself

with a gillette,
in Styria the squirrel

with no body hair was
born. He visited

the psychiatrist,
the psychiatrist told him:

Squat! The lamp on Peugeot
will grow, nails grow.

The lamp on Peugeot grew,
he smashed it.

FOUR, FIVE, SIX

The flag Salò. The master of the
world. It builds itself. It

watches the race. It dies, die! It
dies. It drips itself. It

gives the morsel to the leaf.
It washes the eyes. It

gives the Danube river and the
cotton wool. It sleeps. It

rests. It had her in its neck. It saw
the fly, how it sang. It ran

askance on my four legs. I ran
askance on my six legs.

I stuffed her throat. O
butterflies. We both nodded.

THE LONGING FOR MADNESS

I looked back to see those flat stones.
Water carried it.
When we moved across the valley I lost my bowl.
I won't pull down any wall any more.
Instead of the bowl I'll have to use
my head, it hurts.
My head is black.
On the potatoes there're blue butterflies.
Why don't they pick up those potatoes on the field?
Potatoes are not even a plinth for sculpture.
I have three swords.
All four sides of the world are black.
All four sides of the world crawl into a red
velvet bowl which drowns to the bottom of the sea.
I was killed by the light of Sindbad the Sailor.
I'm gum and iron.
Pears fall on my head, but I don't sense them anymore.
I tore the lower throat of the wolf.
I carried logs of wood on my shoulder.
Then I met the Little Husk.
Don't give tips.
Algae grow in the Andes.
A pail of iron is more valuable then a pail of gold.
Always greasy hands turn the page of the paper.

The mountain chain slips from the frogs' backs.
Jade is inside.
I don't have blood, I have jade.
These are intrigues of letters-peseros
functioning as the agents of genetics.
Blow the cotton wood from your code!
The cotton wood doesn't subsist in paradise.
In paradise the bell subsists
thundering to the ground,
so the platform brakes.

RUMMAGING IN THE YARD, I FOUND

They lifted me with sticks.
I winnowed, with my

belly. But I was neither snake
nor lizard, I was

Tomaž. They dusted my mouth
with white chalk, it

hardens slowly. My snout will be
the same mask as the glove.

Round cut heads, still
hanging. In the

Balkans, from the bags. Also in
Milna, where Stephen

Spender spent summers. Where the
king jumped nude into the sea.

Djurić, Djurić, where are your
bedclothes? You
peed on them, swine, mom's
calf, golden mom's calf.

SLOW MOTION

And here, where are the cremated ones?
Did they die thin-plated? Did imam
tell them? The story goes: first you walk on
white, white snow. Your knees are naked
and you kneel. You don't know what hangs
above: earrings, fishhooks, Chinese
chimes. It rings and tingles. The whiteness is
unbearable, porous and numbered. Then you
step on the silent potato garden.
Potatoes somehow gurgle in the air, named
the knight's field. They turn around. They
glitter. The names shut themselves like
cupboards. Nobody is scratched. And the
farthest away sanskrit flows very tenderly.
But every little brook is relative as at
the end it hurts you like a dentist. The first
language is also the superstition. The origin
is already drawn. And the question if
things are adhered in growing, if names
lead to something, if doggies mate,
all in this white blue rare warm
kasha, the name adepts rightly call
as they call it. The ocean of love and grace.

AFTER THIS NIGHT

In front of a thin plate with round stones.
You say the red pillar appears, the salt

moves. That the red flame breaks out if I
shove away. Such is the consecration

of rocks. To you, to you, water,
water between mirrors. You are the new

young Prince. Confused. Not yet aware
you wetted the cosmos. You'll learn

gradually by paying levies. Janez Bernik
said about Andraž: break his beauty,

his trap is his beauty. The horses, the carriage,
the shawl took care of it. It was given

back to him from Hades. Beauty consumes
him calmly. Silk walls take breath away.

A huge dark man with
radiant eyes dressed in white.
A woman.
A man holding a sphere and a stick.
A woman.
A man holding a sphere and a stick.
A man plowing.
A man carrying a key.
A man holding a snake and a spear.
A woman.
A man holding a sphere and a stick.
A man plowing.
A man carrying a key.
A man holding a snake and a spear.
A woman.
A man plowing.
A man carrying a key.
A man holding a snake and a spear.
A woman.
A man holding a sphere and a stick.
A man plowing.
A man carrying a key.
A man holding a snake and a spear.
A servant holding a whip.
A man who digs, a flautist,
a man with a flute.

I VALUE
MY SEMEN

Storm away, waterfall, storm away.
To rub in one's veins and the movie.

Storm away, waterfall, storm away.
The flesh flows. Staccato flesh.

The hour light. Goethe light.
Her and white stockings.

It's inescapable. Wildly.
The dots on the doge's head.

The central little cats.
The dots on the doge's head.

The central little cats.
To insert the ore in the birch's shine.

Here the house breathes and sleeps.
I value my semen.

GRANDFATHER

I dreamt a huge monument, wrapping itself
with a red wire. Birds didn't peck the stone,
but the interspaces between the wires.
There were no interspaces!
The pores, my grandfather!
Your soul always had the shape of a pear.
You stood on the steep slope above the town.
You held the torch in your hands.
Townspeople started to pour each other with blood,
with the buckets.
Tacitly we went to buy an English dining room.
Everything in the room.
The portrait of young mother and
the silver chest. The salesman told us there's
another town beneath this town.
The cathedral glitters in the sun
under the earth too.
Then you fell.
You crushed the theater.
From your head people started to build
houses. Someone carried your
right thumb to his garden.
And I rushed by car on the dry river.
Your huge monument sealed the treaty.

I kept taking your stony veins from your belly and
kept testing them.
I visited your wife in the hospital
and stuffed the nurses mouths with
five thousand dinar banknotes,
the biggest paper money then.
You were dying.
Not your wife.
Your wife died long ago,
before, in the year one thousand
nine hundred fifty one,
in July,
when mom cried on the terrace.

EAGLE, SQUIRREL, DOE

Mama, I rob.
I ground my pretzels, brothers.
I gave away all my words.
The rose in me rises,
palpates, pulls tight the sweet mass,
caresses, caresses the stone.

You're hugged.
Water trod down
what was to be trodden down.
O ox ball mushroom,
the wound mediatrix.
Bricks, don't contract.
There under the deck, they still burn sailors.

And you: eagle, squirrel, doe,
triangle of all relations, all things:
you're both of us.
Ours are all these white pearls in the sky,
in your sweet, set wide night.
I cut you into your mouth.
Into the cross.

The history of heaven is for everyone.
You don't need to drink anyone's blood,
blood is a censored sperm,
the symbol preserving the temperature
with the sprained picture.
You yourself have to make a decision
to come here or not.
I'm only a speck.
I have no odor, no taste,
nor color, nor shoulder. I'm
not like some whom the crucifixion
could make Jesus Christ.
I didn't steal flowers from there,
when I planted them on the earth.
I'm not on anyone's existing list.
Not an engine who would need to burn
gas or to run between
sun and moon like a Brahmin.
I'm a pure spirit,
without consequence.
With me the history of heaven is untied.
Forever at hand to people,
cats, flies, spiders, roses and lilies.

The fact that a million years ago horses high as a span lived
is such as freshly washed sheets, as a beautiful day.

You run across the plane and you touch the earth.
You run across water and you touch water.
What about a cat, who really falls on her four legs but
can't remain in the air still like a dragonfly?

It's afternoon, it's hot.
The hay is fragrant and dries.

With village skin
you get

with storms. The mop is in
the flower bed of hair.

The bird is canted and runs
on the circumference.

His crown turns. Ends.
I remembered

snails' feelers. Cats
gathered below

a waterfall. They said:
it burned, it will be

bad when we will purr
and they purred.

MA CHARGE N'EST PAS MON MOI, MON MOI N'EST PAS MA CHARGE

I'm the greatest idiot in the world.
I'm the greatest blockhead.
I'm the greatest asshole in the world.

THE MASTER

The bullfinch comes and leaves.
He subdues the cottonwood and leaves.

The elephant's eye aches. My mother's
night aches. Someone, vrooom,

coughs. The savage hears the dog's barking.
He op ens his mo uth.

He mis ses his glas ses. The savage
soaps his dog. Once there'll be

the clematis over the laurel.
Once. Brown shutters, green shutters.

Ay, the cradle, ay, the volt.
Ay, the baby, ay, the bet.

Ay, the gulp, ay, the grebe,
ay, happiness.

THE DANUBE

These memories are candy. Candy.
Wake up, dog. Get lost snarling.
These shadows exist in morning,
when the space between dark and light is

not oblique, not differently warm, not
differently good. His bunch of roses is
garish and reminds us of a dog rose tea.
The cardinal drank a dog rose tea. Sometimes

he manipulated provinces, freely, cynically.
Sometimes he pecked them thoughtfully,
mournfully. There are many trucks along
the Danube, loading dust. Drivers are

jumping in the mud among ducks. People
sing on trains, they're stained and unshaved.
The sun gets stuck in them like hayforks.
Near Drava river there are many umbrellas and

sunshades. Many yellow flowers, cars with
unturning wheels. Isn't it naïve to take bread
into nature? Isn't there any higher instance
so we can be indignant and complain?

EHM

I glide and love you, up to your
toes. I'll eat you and kill you.

I see green windows. I ironed
moths. I restore graves

to life. Your tongue, with the snow.
In cascade. Look, the eyes are

mantras. You're sculpture
coagulating. Then,

in the lake, I can swim butterfly
stroke and set a record.

You wind around me. You wind
around you. The rain falls too,

and I see the sun. And even when
the sun shines I see the sun.

CHRIST'S HEART

Christ's heart split in two pieces
and rolled at both ends

of the towel. Instantly the corridor
was ash grey. Try to love one

another! People shrieked in a panic.
Too late! Waiters broke in with

silver trays, court hawks flashed off
their shoulders. Who had truly

heard the noise of trays, leisurely made,
moving in the corridor from

one to the other stone plate had
to lubricate himself three

summers and three winters more. Then
everything was OK with people.

RUSSIANS

Kind lobes as punched
cups. It gurgles, gurgles,

rain. On the Rhine bank I rolled rock
with blue copper. I lunched

with Rejn's ex-wife. She cried.
Harsh is my hill, my

eye is bloodshot. My hair was
plucked by spiders. While I

sneeze, grottos open. Wild
game airs inside. My juice

is all in white. I'm all in white.
I cry and take small

steps, anthems roar below the
black soil. And you?

MY PRICKY WANTS TO FUCK!
MY PRICKY WANTS TO FUCK!

O juice, I see you in yellow blinkers.
Caress a bit my little prick, caress me!
This, that I'm forbidden to utter your name,
is a dreadful chain. I'll bite through it
with my teeth. Look, I give you this calf.
And hills and woods and the river. I'll
scrape you a barbell from the moon and make
you an oar from it. The rose sleeps. O Carnival,
where oaks are falling. The wine flows over
your head, I collapse in your rowboat and fall
asleep. I put dry twigs under the star and pour over
gasoline and then push, push this Italian from
the bridge so you'll hear the gargling and see
how the man drowns. (O mummy! Tugo!)

JUSTICE

For Peter Trias

You, coming on foot to Pasadena with diamonds
under your skin, disguised as a muzhik,
as you fell out with Kerensky,
living like Tolstoy,
among olive and orange plantations,
your granddaughter Joan
wedded a man who continues you
and drenches you with Ivan the Terrible.
He swam across steppes, kingly gentle,
detached, tender like a doe, a murderer,
until he didn't name and restored the orthodoxy:
Greece. Peter looks like Andraž.
He's taller. More nervous. More innocent.
At four in the morning washed with the new color
of his eyes—the blue—mellow and young like a woman.
I eat your body in Hampstead, 2 Windmill Hill.
This house is the altar. I'm the plunderer and the son,
nailed into the chain,
trembling from bliss.
Tall and tanned from the sun I feel
how you crumble me like bread.
How you are putting me down for food,
you, the highest, silent miracle.

MICHAEL PUKES IN FRONT OF THE HOTEL BELLE STELLE

In the mountains the black pope lies.
His nose is sideways. Quick! The stroke!

Here's El Greco's influence. Toledo
pours through his Eustachian

tube. Radetsky's horses piss
in the court later! Later!

O thighbone, whistle! Wonder at
the wonder. *Tra poco vengo su.*

So, we looked at it. Did the stains
remain? Or, they fell upon

immediately, covered everything with
a tilled ground and built a city.

That count Orgaz was the devil.
Beetles de-leafed themselves.

the passion of the mob, kernels of logos
the god of green rhymes, of fur lined coats
breasts of a young snake, snails' membranes
hunger is blood, hunger is power
colors, the skin of golden blacks
dead guards, hands of lacquered idlers
hoods, killed eros's gleam
smooth butterflies, the cloths of his blood
he appeases from far away, he shines from far away
close by he walks, devoted pilgrims
the circle of grass, the linearity of wood
fires on meadows, burdens of pasture
how dreadfully the mouth opened
berries of the conflagration, the luster of sacrifice
cubus, folds for sheep of the wounded god, the sea of
body hair, the frightful transparency of white paper
large barking fields, smooth white planks
how the son rots, the soft skin of doe
how the water flows near, the cartilage pineapple
hunters, the wedge between windows ajar
calm window panes, penetrating window panes
seven layers of troy, the burning of candles
the laying of scotch tape, heavy hanged balls,

of the ellipse, angles of bent wires
greasy fins, the axes of sun and venus
invented lines of body transmissions
the trouting of planes, cameramen of the soil
evenly shaven animals, hot mess tins
mom among tall wheat, shower under us
jumping with worn out cardboard,
the diagram on the columns
calm down, make love and kill
calm down, embroidered beetle

THE SUNS

I don't hear.
Always at the start.
I'm hearing only detonation.
Honey crisps and a bee licks.
The light rolls past barrels,
it calms, it hews.

The middle finger, the ring finger,
the forefinger on the nape of the neck,
backs, mountains of thumbs on the edges of the jaw.
Wrench out the head from the neck.

I don't hear the sentence.
I just stuff the cave.

I'm dividing shadows.
I'm hardening white wax.

I wait that all wood putrefies.
It shakes. It calls me in sleep.

It tears. I have my wires in the sun.
Fused with blueness,
I wipe my juice from your neck.

PELLEAS

Pelleas guesses:
an elephant, I don't know, a thief,
children's jubilance, I don't know, an anchor.

Whatever you say, Pelleas
has its taste, its hour,
its noble color.
The latent noble hips
of the enemy and of the friend.

PEGASUS GETS TATTOOED

I put the fish in the baking tin and looked
if the moon has eyebrows.
I carried the iodine on my shoulders.

No one robs the linear one.
You, birds, also not.

As a messenger I waved on a moist
blanket on my profusely sweaty horse.

THE FISHS

The fishs, like dark vases, the ships of lightning,
breathe like dolphins.
All fishs. All mirrors.
All times. All buddies flow together.

The fishs, which are a heavenly hoop,
slice home into dry powder
like giant spiders.
Time goes by without the mind.
Because of weight, because of flash,
it rushes into tusks,
the lowly grown-up boy.

To swim, to be highbred.
To wash, to wash, to wash the wage.
The door opens.
The kiosk is closed.
The truck transports.
I don't know what transports.
The man has a light green jacket.
I'm tired. Blissfulness hurts me all over.
The child fell asleep.
Devices are.
I don't want to fly away.
I want to eat sand.
We walked the Chinese Woods
in Central Park.
I was drunk after the first cigarette.
I shriek myself.
I grow into spruce.
Deluge will come.
I don't want to go on.
You should live.

The throbbing of your heart strikes my forehead.
You're calming down. You sleep and
wince.

You're my fortress, my cross, my
altar. I cannot, I cannot, I cannot
live without you. If I want to escape,

you crush me, you don't pimp me
out. Ruthless, cruel pasha.
Frightened boy, whom I

nauseate. You don't *get* these
feathers. These shrieks and the power
that evaporates. You're hurt by

consumption. You flow away,
so I must brand you. You suck me
like a magnet. You breathe me

and if we're not alloyed, you humble
the same way I do. I'm ages on the
lookout to be faithful to this cleft

that nourishes your datum. You
nail me and soften me, you make me
a deranged Jew. But the monster

thwarts your loot. He sets it in your
folds. Do you remember? Circular,
circular. Will you show me his grave? My

brains and my marrow feed your
bronze blood with passion. I die gladly
for your battle with time, my soul.

ALTAR

On the small, almost completely overgrown
gravel path, I found a stone. It was red.
Far in the south it rained. I wondered if the rain
will come here. I wanted to wet the stone. I stored
it under my shirt. It rolled around my waist. Even in the south
it stopped raining. I'd roast a
rabbit if I found it. The floor swayed. I drew
the crown into the sand, but couldn't
put it on my head. I took the red stone
and placed it in the middle. The stone
traveled through the earth. The crown spun
round and hissed. The path grew wider then
narrowed instantly. Two arrows, shot into my
body from both sides, touched their heads.

Foam of a hut,
lava target.
Have pity,
have pity.

Not a balance,
nor bread,
nor a pine forest I know,
that would glitter so strongly in the moonlight.

In the black chest
the housewife lay in flour.
Young Mary has mustaches above
her upper lips.

How fanatically she kisses the hare!
He'll die of overdose
and nod with his ears down.
Mother hare will wash him,
She'll try to give him aspirin through his white little teeth.

I stepped on a frigate.
I had a bundle on my shoulders.
I greeted the captain,
I said to him, good day, guy.

STRIPPER

the stripper jumps upwards falls
on the floor and twists in feigned
before-dead spasms distorting her face
below and above she rolls herself in
two or three folds then with all her
limbs explodes in several directions
her eyes burn her cigarette burns
the audience gets earnest now the stripper
is on her navel now again on her feet
the audience starts yerking on their seats
now she's soft like a salad now torpid
like fulmaris glacialis some more young
guests in the back stand up and stare

THE WHEEL

O, like a little puppy I slept on the floor,
washed myself in the window.
I didn't trust your honeyed heart.
We ate breakfast when you
smelled like the Urmother of hours,
mortally dangerous to me.
I tied you up.
You forbade me to steal horses.
They'll come by themselves!
They'll come by themselves!
And I smacked my lips.

Only you are here
to burn you and forget you,
my property.
Collapsing wet brown houses,
how should I get up.
How should I drink your gulps
in this thick, poisoned
sea air.
You by yourself broke your eyes and
pulled out your
scent with your rattle, your
banal black moan.
You give a damn what happens to me.

Come, break me, reduce me. I'm becoming
the family milk bowl. The siren will
kill me. Tear her dress off like Virgil to make her

a fat, abashed, gelatine. I'm mashed by rocks.
She devours me like a tempest, she devours
the tattered flag. I'm an ice cream cone

melting in the child's belly. Smashed
grapeskins. The yawning of sybaritic gazelles.
As an elephant I squirted. As a leopard I

squatted on the cow's heart, the big one, at the edge
bordered with pearls. Bamboo was stuck in
the heart's small nooks which on the other side

kept opening like mouths that had just passed
through the gelatine. The arrow, the wing,
the fish fins, the diamond nib of my liquified

brain. This makes the empire. Lust.
Appoint the sirens in the valleys, but I
swallow you out of myself. I enjoy

you out of myself. And I want more.
More, more, more, still more, 'til the pain
with it's heel squeezes my soul like toothpaste

from my throat. To have a good cry again and to
tremble, to shake like an overhead machine
and to sob. To need you. To need you.

He took a thin wire and
cut me in half.

The towel is red. We
saw the woodpecker.

I'll catch cold. I'll sleep
here. I don't want

to go anywhere. You
can use

complicated words. I
won't. I already

long ago
ensured my

right to put my head
anywhere I want.

THE NEWS

The news changed. The dust of butterflies
is like the ceiling of bees. The belly above the sun
is the crime and the punishment. If now it tugs
me down, it will crash me into the boiling

lava. I don't want it. I want still to climb. Here
the air is so rare, I cough, it pushes me up. The hard
body cannot go through the hard body, such
a miracle is like a dirty rag and undeserved. I try

to dive and pierce the glowing mass, but I
cannot. I try to dive. Right, so when it rains
and doesn't sizzle, when I lean forward and my

legs overthrow because of gravitation, I will
know that I can let it go. With a ton of lead
the air will rustle like the propeller of a steamboat.

RED
MUSTANG

A milk tooth, sculptors, grey mold.
Hey, little twig in the soup, dipped and

heated. Your hair was skimmed as such was
the fashion of glaciers. They shoved you

in lime. First the edge of Mozart's
sleeve started to fry. My room at Paros

was smeared with that lime. Why do you not
resist? Why do you accept everything?

Why do you fall asleep so blessed? You
crawl away. You always lock me.

I never lock the lower door.
Measure this pan.

It grows by your palm tree.
Brunelleschi's little wall. The wall.

ANNA NICOLE SMITH

Rascals salt a salad and use fish. They throw
a hamster on foil. The hamster

wakes up and speaks. At this corner?
At this corner, you say, a monologue on

acid? And what if you'd lose your
cap? Let's say you'd forget it. We would all be

pale. Young male cannot lose his cap. Did you
see what a layer of ice they drew around her

lips? No one believed she was like this. She
wasn't concerned about his millions. She loved

him. And you roll and roll and breathe and
write. In the woods moles and holes and pressed

skyscrapers live. He lifted his body and started
to spit in his mouth as if he were a chameleon.

THE BOATS

I'm religious.
Religious as a wind or scissors.
An ant eats, she's religious, flowers are red.
I don't want to die.
I don't care if I die, now.
I'm more religious then the dust in the desert.
Children's mouths are round. My eyes are
a syrup, the cold drips from it.
Sometimes I think nettles stung me, but they
didn't. I think I'm unhappy, but I'm
not.
I'm religious.
I'll throw the barrel in the river.
If bees would rush after my face, I would scratch
my face with my hand and I would see
again.
I don't get upset.
My soul presses like crowds press the door.
When I die oxen will graze the grass the same way.
Houses will glimmer the same way.

STEAM

If you wanted the silk you drew it.
This hydrate booms.

It's on the chin.
It's on the chin.

It's Tadzio.
It's Tadzio.

I go to swim, Te Deum.
The juice of those frozen.

Silenzio Maria, pray for us, chiseler
in front of the cameras. We hail

the master. We have grated salted
flocks. Cross the algae.

Cross the algae.
Cross the capillaries.

Svarun roars,   (God Svarun)
Svarun roars,

braid sings,
braid sings.

Invent the blue vehicle on the blue water,
the yellow vehicle on the blue water.

Small flags, small flags, I touch the rope
binding flags.

You are you.
Smooth and sculpted.
You are you.

Is the bran nuclear?
Is the tall sand in the trunk?

Two mathematicians under light.
The white pearl leaning on the playground.

You shake, it purls,
you carry Vipava river on your shoulders.

LAZY, ASTONISHED R. CRUMB

Sarah Bernhardt,
in panic of Isadora Duncan,
jumps from tram to tram,
from taxi to taxi.
Ruffian Yesenin counted
less than women, irrespective of
his muzhik taste.
What kind of glory is cultivating
kale to the oppressed,
R. Crumb asked me after his talk
at the Chicago Art Institute.
Well, they may lose their burdens,
I guess.
They have an incredible instinct for moisture.
They're infallible there,
I said timidly,
almost robbed of my
utmost sacred conviction.

PARATAXIS

Somebody nailed me like an ant, like
a cripple leaning on a Barnes & Noble

paneling, wavering in delight. Storms
roar and gyrate. Their fins are like

whale's fins, they will annihilate my life.
Whales will annihilate my life.

I give it gladly for what I experienced.
I give it gladly for what I experience

now. The sun returned, I thought it went
out. I thought I lost it. I'm happy.

The storm doesn't end. I'm like a flower
leaping if getting a drop of water.

Nothing slows down. Like cats we're
thrown into a box on God's arms.

Lord, I ask you humbly, push me away!
Liquidate my head and my wrists.
Let me be a torso vomiting blood.
Enough for me.

Let my head and palms look at each other outside of me.
Let them be kicked, let them spin round above the fountain.
Let someone with a lighter come closer.
Let them shoot in the sky above the cathedral.

Someone with a blue garlic—ricochet—
soaps the doorman. Should we
help him?

All corpses falling
under my bunker
will be called

asslicks.

STONE PINES

The knife on the neck. The shame.
The shame. The supple shame.

Dipped in Ave Maria. The knife on the
neck. The shame. The shame.

The supple shame. Dipped in Ave
Maria. The thyroid gland.

The boat. The pin huts.
Jamaica. The gear on the lynx's

stem. The lame ones. The beasts.
The lame ones. The villains with flakes

of moisture. The round stone.
For Piggy Bank.

Piggy Bank.
Fucked!

the rolling, trees glue debauchery
the dead Christ, a cavalry, white nun's handkerchiefs
a wrinkled canvas, he looks vigorous and barefoot
splendid and killed, handsome with dark brown soles
on the right the typical iconographic logs, a little cat
Tobias with a hump on his apex, with his hand on the chest of
    logos' march
ladybugs carry messages, a gentlewoman plays chess
the meeting point of poachers
Tyssen with Giovanna Tornabuoni
we fix the frame with a screw, with threads
with nickeled pulley bought in a hardware store
you'll be buried beneath, heated cavalry
torn down by colonnades with profiles
algae, scents, Moses in the arms with a model of
poison food and indifference of lucidity
two young fiancés with a horse and a mirror
dry yellowish corpse, blue millimeter paper
what do you sing? a lullaby? a meditation in the chasuble?
palm trees? birds above the sea and crocodiles?
how the door develops?
how does Don Fernando Nino de Guevara sleep?
the calendar, the calendar, towers, a wet grass
the smelly flesh and the treatise about sanctity of the family

papal nuncios, a tall willow tree, the blood softly running away
the celebration, the bread on viola da gamba
in the antechamber the dog
in the fine woven basket little spoons lacquered with faith
the rolling, the passion of cattle, of skaters, seducing the rhythm
having in the hand pornography and trembling
flowers, plankton, Christmas cribs and colored rocks
this gives us the power to breathe, this gives the power to sense
    the pen
let us peel little Flemish girls with sharp scent

Majority of us were washed, we partied.
Windows were closed. I waited for

a ring. Hearts languished and left. Centaur
invites. The steps are varnished. It

blows, we sink. There are unopened
packages and letters in the smaller

room. A horse means status. A horse
always means status. Shoes lie

asunder. They remind me of my mom.
From which sack did you drink?

Not from mine? Leaves obey. The sky
is hasty. The darkness penetrates

deep. With you in me, I'm in total bliss.
Grasshoppers are green and thunderous.

BRIGHTLY CARVED INTO HIS NAME

To fuck Šalamun and chain him to himself.
To perforate, to kill, and only then throw
away. Let him amuse his own crickets. Flesh
destroys the Castle of His Mass. He should be

my dog, my madly enamored Swabian. Let him
slither. His snout should lick the salt that
I command. Let him cool in the name of hate.
Let first his shadow pine away, before he's

crushed by himself. Let him leave this world
without a drop of water. Let my sword impale
everyone of his suite into their paunch. Let

his monsters gurgle their final breath and
henceforth multiply only as my fathers. I will
disfigure all his orbit. My master plan is Karlo.

THROUGH THE OPEN WINDOW BREAKS A MAN OF NOTE, THROUGH THE OPEN WINDOW BREAKS A SYMBOL.

Lose the luster, heavenly sweetmeat.
Let an ant eat you.

Do, drive.
Pick up shirts.

GENERATION

Did the stone fall into water?
Did the fish open its mouth just below
the surface and suck midge?
Did you touch the white wall-tiles of telegraph poles?
I sink into myself as if into a mountain.
I caress the coalmine handcars,
the white shoulders
of warm muffs.
Let's exchange, runs every seduction.
You give me passion, I give you
enormous ping-pong table's throat,
airplanes on it, the navy. The mountain's
mouth that will vomit them. The ultimate
speed that will petrify enemy soldiers. It is
accomplished.
We have to train salt pillars to blow
their mind back to them, to pawn them as
scenery. We know their eye dribbled out.
The diamond on its apex generates fire.
Look! That's why I can step behind your shoulder
and dictate to you the desire, the hunger, the picture.
That's why I can bowl you precisely
as the dark fresh young king,
to entrench you as my gentle paw.

ALLOYING

Give me your eyes, stop before my eyes.
It was weird in the night. You boiled

my lungs. The liquid in them became black,
you were like three hundred thousand

Persians marching toward a dry tree. You
amalgamated me, enchained me, melted,

chained me again. The haft was contrite. There
was a tempest. Green hydrochloric acid

poured over hundreds of thousand of ants.
I didn't interpolate. Branches burnt in

a flash. Am I snuffed? Do I not exist? I saw
thy garden. Moist leaves first smoked like

stable manure, then moved. The single giant's eye
watching. It's true. I'm reckless. No more.

ION IN THE WOODS

The skill is a brook
and a small thin man. Aphrodite
stood up from the filling.

I'm cold here. I go in.
Who has a music ear, let his
bindweed pale.

First they pinched me through
the door. In jail they threw my keys
across the street.

I slept with the girl, not with
the customs woman, and when I've
eaten grapes, the rest

I threw in the trash.
How do we call it?
The stem?

Penholder?
Father of small balls?
Green stalk?

The neighbour woman rattles
about her daddy, I drink
wine.

I see sex I eat sex roofs are soaked by rain

THE
NIGHTINGALE

Hogs, nightingales, ponds in Gabrče,
bald madam Tončka at the door.
My cousin glues lips of movie
stars, Sergej trains judo.

Are cows related to mister Toni
who was my nonno's clerk?
When he stepped to the threshold
he sang: O, Parigi, città de Dio.

My nonna said: take him off
the desk. Nonno said:
Signor Toni is a decent lad,
let him think he's the nightingale.

TOADSTOOL

You're my cogged little frog,
a belly, a caramel, an adder.

Grown up I breathe.
The sound heats me. It's

5:11. I gave money to the beggar.
A mousetrap captures tree and

ore. You who sleep, wake the
fuck up. Let's go. Gloved herds wait

for us. Cows get milked. Pittsburgh
has many valleys. Many tears.

Much of what, what? Worms crawl into
face. You who sleep, wake up.

Let's go. The crown hails. Someone
knocks at the door. Don't open.

who are you? the effect of well fed herds?
well read towers, plunderers
who are you? lead will come, from the sky the day
grass mould, waterfall from the rock
the lieutenant with a mask, with chunks the note
remember: doormen, the carousel on the hill
wine with the cork, with the eyes the gas
marches, the ribbons of aluminium
an auction, with the son the barge
silent: birdlime grows, the wound with the good name montaigne
a small circle, a shade, a building, a helper
el farat, the nimbus, the rubicon
who are you? hands made of square fields
the food, the seer, the scope of millers wives
a predicate made of rosemary
from the toad, miss švalba
how are you grown up together? we planted the mulberry tree
the sun comes up, the squire out of bushes
the long, long, for appearance's sake smoothly
placed stick around the use
of salust clement, the fighting cornelius's squire
the greenland steamboats
kiddo, kiddo, kiddo
the bet, the ore drives in the open

the leek, the blanket, the process, cornelia again
the doorman in the hill, the power of fingers, the crown of the neck
where are the precise formulations of the straight soft movements?
what he attains I chew up, patina glues on
the sea, the bomb, gray mouse, the penalty kick
grilled penny, from the earth the snow is lazing down,
roots out papers, the hold-up, cornelia again
otto? du otto? ja, ich munser
mingle religiously, let flowers have the smallest surface possible
the smoke, the shore, the kerchief, the skiing wavers
the inner balance, the strong man
there's the neck, there are goods, he adhered horizontally
gravitation burns through,
gravitation burned through

THE BIRTH OF THE POET

The warm calf's belly is on his
forehead. Flies buzz and crawl
into his mouth. He closes
the powerplant. He intercepts

the raft with the oar. He hits
the cherries, prepares the sling. An ox
falls like a bronze, father doesn't. Rice is
stuck on his neck, behind his forehead.

There are rings in the cement. Their soft
wood drowns into his flame. Muscle
destroys his face. It's scribbled. It tortures

itself and stares. His entrails are spread
as if he knew where the birds would go.
The warm calf's belly is ripened for command.

Your poor scrotum.
Measure is the passworth.
Among horses and in army
blankets a dead boy is wrapped.

The continuation is a paper
wounded with a pin,
spurting your lost bid for life.

WHITE FIELD

Whoever doesn't set asunder the mouth
at the monkey will leave the scene to tailors.

Man! Use me more frequently!
We have only seventy-six days left

to be at this distance. After that there will be
water between us, dreadful water.

Paths are for snails. Ears are for mantras.
And what about clay which flashes, which is

not silverware in the eyes? What about immortal
warm yawning? Gazelles knit little gloves

for their kids and sons. I peal and rush. I'm your
ancestor, but you're my ancestor too. You

came on bike. You were uneasy. The animal
overheats and is astonished. Fold the ladder.

dreadful feasts, roads, fields
peasants, dark coiffures, lilac smells
I hear the noise, clear irruption
Alexander, I closed my mouth, when the sun went down
fairytales, convicts in brown clothing
ante murale cristianitatis, urns with oil
the rainbow, draw the blossom and you'll be revered
the focus, the burning bush, the heron of herons
we'll break the door in the sun, dip bread in the earth
lid paths above the evening, racetracks
pierce water with the mallet, burn the world's face
leaves, a passion of the tongue
happy animals, happy beasts
they circle, they speak, mothers of dust
the pilgrimage of sin, yards of white mouths
here, by my death, everything springs
grill fish, dwarves, squeeze house corners in your bags
the moon sleeps, carpets
frozen snow, I see blood on the fur coat
I see iron grids, Persian cats
I don't want to die in the steppe, I don't go on
I want to be killed by a cicada, the earth's womb

GUILT AND PASSION

Town traffic vehicles are green.
The moon is full. Watch out! I set you
a trap. With my greediness, not
your fatality I struggle. My pneuma
rolls you in spaces that cannot be grasped
with your senses. I'm wounded. Watch
out. I see far. It's true what they
whispered. I'm the lord who disposes
the gleam of others. Watch out. I'm
warning you. You pushed aside
your wounds because you fell asleep
in the crystal. I give to seize. To open
you and to pierce through you. To
break the base of time, as this is right.

Silver wings will call in the air,
hunters will eat in the air.

Stigmata are drawn with technical expedients,
the bird who dies upset is an apparition.

Birds ruin cities, they ruin the sea,
the wind ruins the foam, disperses it.

Son, you're strong,
survive!

THE VISIT

The brown color of Teotihuacan is circling.
The sun presses grapes, crumbles the membrane.
Shadows are lying down as a taint on a young skin.
There's no fish.

Toys recede as they'd sled from walls.
A pastel senses a punch, a hollow one.
I watch illumination,
I think they are crates for hares.

Jesus (Hesús) turns the radio on.
Blurs roll into bumps and vaporize.
Lopsided jeans are visible from the moon.

Entrance, exit, the same direction.
Innumerable ladles, they pacify heads
with red eyes. Voice, the air, the teethridges.

o

Water in a bright metal bag round the neck of the animal.
A feather on pine tree needles on steep ground.
Let my arm overgrow into roots.
I see one part of a roof, a piece of roof.

I'm waking up, the sun is sliding.
A fluff sprouts to the clouds, it dies.
Let the stone's shadow fall to the ground before the stone.
The sound thickens.

I draw a line with my knife around the mill in the turf.
The star is waiting to be crushed.
It doesn't fall. It waits to fall.
August. The dust hardens.

o

The seed of intelligence snows on the face of the doe.
It washes it, it wounds it.
The three columns of the transmission lines in the woods.
A blueberry, it doesn't exist.

Fingers freeze.
There is fire in the huts.
The seed of intelligence scatters hush on the sand.
The picture is hard.

I'm shaking off my shoes.
Below the eaves I see water.
Smoke is undisturbed.
Gold peels from the windows of the house.

o

If not then if it won't then
if a crown if a blossom
a gnarl opens a gnarl opens
I have a cap I have a cap
the river brings colors
I hear I hear the dark curtain goes
to the left it reatreats as if I'd watch it through
rain fingers cry I hear the servant
speaking I watch the cigarette smoke
one threshold more and I'll munch
I munch I'm lost I'm lost it stirs me
like polenta I contract I expand
contracting expanding I go round
to give them a place in myself
they're like dwarves many dwarves
they're of pastels colors my woolen pullover
is made out of smoke I didn't swallow
anything no plant no powder I don't need
any plant any powder the machine started to

shudder it doesn't want to if I'm carried away
from the riverbed it hurts me everything hurts
me from happiness me Buddha sitting in
the little caves of my ears

o

the world travels in clouds and flowers
who sees knows
all is the same all is one
it is soft is soft and pierces
until now I called the gods now
they came they are here in me with me
we are colors we are colors colors
powder such a strange powder as
rain the molasses happiness are molasses
thinning it becomes scarce I'm tired I'm lazy
I'm tired lazy blessed I can't figure it out
I'm awashed exploded the heart survived

it seemed it will TTAK! stop now it is as
a cauliflower's blossom on every
leaf's millimeter there are huge cities
shone upon with light now I can
crawl in between swim and breathe
so that all children all grown ups

all people can all fall asleep in beauty as in
water everything is what it is

o

I put epitaphs into the machine as I
wait for my brothers once I died on X
I went up from downstairs to upstairs in
die Spitze where I was annihilated then I started
to crawl apart alive now it is different now I
travel on the surface twelve years of staring into
whiteness is the school but now it's no
not needed anymore the school this is made
rather very simply like if you'd jump from a horse
stand up from the wheel open the door
cross the threshold you're greeting everybody
you can talk at the same time some
kind stupidities it doesn't matter in sum
you go completely and naturally through
and in and out without dramas tragedies
doomsday or punishment these walks
are from color to color color to color
eternally in all directions —
they're infinite —
of the cross

Your little bones love
my little bones.

Excellent feeling. Flowers
grow above us. People

trip. Some have wet
shoes. They light

candles and munch. They're
cute. Our little bones—

total kooks. If you
dig them out

they don't scare anybody.
They're sacrum.

Ossa sacra,
mamma mia.

TORCELLO, CALLED "THE BARBARIAN," RETREATS

The protopapered starings we destroyed greasily like.
Okay, okay, okay, okay.

I stood on ice.
My mother went to the market with
a basket full of flowers to sell it
to the rich ones.
She didn't sell it.
I turned my palm.
Enough for the storm to pull down the beams
hewed by my grandfather
And my mother still has
a young, lean body
pleasing to horses and peasants.

I REVEAL MYSELF AND I HAVE A PURE SOUL

are you serious

serious

do you pray for every one you destroy

I pray for every one I destroy with love

do you stomp them

in the mouth and between the eyes
in the back of the neck

don't you think it's dangerous to destroy yourself too

sure in some sense it is dangerous
I constantly have to measure distances

what are you doing with kids

I seduce them

do you seduce a lot of them
relatively a lot

but recently the resistance mounts
why do you think

the higher standard of living probably and because
the new generation is more rested

Your eyes are blue, boy sphinx.
Your eyes are black.

You own an Apple computer.
Gods like us.

I'm disappearing. I attained all.
It's stopped. You need an ID.

They don't give you cigarettes
without the ID. Paws chased you.

Brown didn't get you.
Please, fisherman. Don't get

scared. I'm throbbing. I don't
like it. I have stiff knees.

I don't believe this happened
while you worked. You allowed me.

I wish all whores to be spit on thorns
and catch tetanus.

Whores are awesome.

IN THE MOVIE HOUSE

Let's say there're three hundred bones in your ankle,
I'd break them into three hundred thirteen,
eat them, bite them through, here and there
spit some out, bite some through twice.
My teeth would reel, but enamel keeps
the sun, keeps it in its hands, doing utz! utz!

Lucretius grabbed my arm and lead me
to the spot where he went nuts. I watered little
drums right away and entangled the Sava river
with knitting needles. I putrefied a small soup,
dismembered seven towels. There, He —The
Terrible — burnt on the stake, squatted too.
My god, I beat him up his ass. Puff, puff, but
no one had heard a thing. Now here, I'm flooded
with flowers by cumin. Even Tarkovsky appears.
Now I will suck you with my thumbs, mold
you like clay with my horns, till he'd vaporize and
see into what and where I've traveled to. Into
honor. Into white birch trees. Into the pouch
used for bread. I hung around the world a lot,
frothily crushing the mountain range. With no
avail, with no day's pay, sticky are my laws.
I protected an elephant as much as I could,
stared at the back of the horse. Joshed the others,
now, too, tested spring mattresses. Kept
gulping nirvana. Loosened feathery leaves,
wrapped the emperor into a roll. To not let my
senses perish, to gallop without a break.

GRANNY

O my Tomilay,
come back,
don't untie your hair.
Don't forget the golden doe
beneath birch leaves.
Shoot only in self defense.
Do you always give enough to beggars?

My horse had heard it too.
This was the voice of my dead granny.
Let's stop, horsey.
I'm really sick probably.
Where do I ride after all?
The solar discus?
What did the phantoms who tire me so
really want? Might these skeins be
some head offices liking me
alone in the mountains?
And who will put his body
on the paper for Metka's
drawing?

I'm hexed, horsey.
Again I've done a silly thing.
When I open the door, I say don't
ask. Red Hand Brotherhood
totally bewilders me,
you'll read in the poem.
I choked and I feel awfully
guilty that the bull yesterday almost
killed you.

Here, my hand!
Draw it.
Let it be red to remember,
although I'm still
furious at those little Martians.

And you should know to be thankful to my
Granny. We won't
visit more churches for you to
have fun with Christs in
violet velvet Bermuda
breeches.

WINDY
BUT
NICE

A petrified face danced
with ants, little ants

kicked themselves in hips. We listened.
We watched—a vista.

We climbed but our hands
rattled. Our shoes go askew.

The nets—we anointed
firemen—and below surface

there were strikes—
the sun suppressed the clouds.

It beamed rubber like and yellow.
Birds were satisfied. Palm trees were

satisfied. Dogs barked in
pieces. In crackling pieces.

STEAMBOATS

The light, falling from the wheels on the great rivers,
is still rustling. To let you take your shoes off, to let you
sneak in your sleeping bag and leave this outside.
You sleep in the open, on the dew, on the frost.

Landscape, o landscape, the sheer flat land, it slides.
And in the morning, how warm you are. How the fluff
heats you. You're moist only on your lips, on your
eyelashes. At the Saratoga Springs' post office the

ladies on frescoes promenade with their parasols,
dogs walk up and down and the artist gets some
bread. Roosevelt. New Deal. Sleep on thick

white bear's fur. The driver will drive you to buy
paper. Do you sense how I take off your
boots? Every poem I start to write like this.

WHITE PEOPLE

I traveled to Alaska with my
mum. We ate pizza

each of us in his or her cabin. Polar
bears were sitting on the cliffs,

they couldn't reach us. The path
to Alaska is long. Less

interesting than generally thought.
Ron, who was also fishing

in Alaska, showed me
how you throw

a black man into the sea, so he
perishes and dies. If

anywhere, there's still a place
for white people.

They lived together in paradise.
Up to the gorge of the clinical chicken.

Up to a *woman in first six to eight weeks after
giving birth.* We have one word

for such a woman in Slovenian. A certain
kind of grey fracture. Screes

are menaced with salt.
Ey, ey, in the woods I'd walk on you.

THE SPINDLE SHOULDN'T COME IN THE WINDOW

Carmelite nuns are barefoot.
The spindle is afraid of the peacock.

Carmelite nuns seize the blue sheet,
they lift it above their heads and howl.

I'm a Carmelite nun, I'm
a Carmelite nun. All four of them.

On all four corners. Then they run
barefoot on the soft grass with

the taut blue sheet. They put it on
the grass. Their feet palms jet.

We hear gurgling. They're not Carmelite
nuns anymore, dipped in the water.

They cry and become dried
chamomile, irrespective of.

THE WINDOW FROM WHICH ONE CAN SEE THE MOST SHIPS

To newsboys, along their throats, towels that will wash
    themselves like
Silent Night fall tenderly.

THE WORK ON A PLATFORM

Pearls of white queen bee,
huge white gull plane above the lavender field,
above the houses, factories along the river,
thirty meters tall shiny thin plate
half a kilometer long,
there the brain pours onto paper.
The wind swings steel strings.
To the wood—the little boat—you can't strip off
gray concrete. You pull off body hair, puff
blowballs. Would a ship keel, ribs, stand
on the street? Does the worker mixed
in concrete look like the black man from
Madagascar? He has black skin,
it shines like iguana skin. Is the white
crocodile falling on both flanks and
fluttering, beating his apples, still
the iguana? You make PhD and you want
to go into the dinosaur's keel.
You take chocolate from his mouth,
the machine drops little pads and you watch
them rally on the lawn. Everyone has to bring
fifteen tubes. Three rucksacks. Twenty, up to
twenty-seven strings. All of them have
taut muscles, all of them have the same

gestures. Do they display or put together
their bycicles? Will they go somewhere?
Why don't they give some work to
the shoeshine man? In the Smithsonian
there're the longest bones. Some sweet juice,
some *prosseco* in rags is available for tourists.
I have pupils in my mouth. The gaze goes
on the picture. The skin will rehabilitate.

I know this Hopi jewelry
around your waist:
this is the sadness of Pontormo.
Santa Fe:
with my hand in the junkie's mouth,
I step in the morning
wounded glimmering mother pearl.

Grieves,
piled up like grey blocks on grey attics of parallel sky.

Sheep,
your little furs lean on apples.

Why did it ring and there're no goblets on the table?
Did a squirrel meet a dwarf and fight him for the cap?
Let's go to the terrace and sing in a choir:
the night, you're lazy, we're hungry!

The beginning is the end.
In the middle is the cramp or whirlpool.
Hours have rained on us like orange potatoes.
I have put the orange potato into the bank
beneath the orange desk.

We're all food.
And don't be afraid of me because I'm a glutton.
What a glutton eats sails like a dragon.

Why is it only the boat that moves on,
why doesn't sand move on too?

Fish, which are cardboard,
mastiffs, owned by the king.

I told you a long fairytale,
fell asleep before it ended.

Bčka is a little kitty that falls into milk.

Živžav walks along the street and takes a bar of soap with him.
He comes to a fence and forgets the bar of soap at the fence.

MINERS

Palms burn.
Palm trees burn.
Triangles burn.

A horse paws on the sand like a girl from
the north touching nettles.

Gold caves open.
Water freezes.
God's eye swills little brooks
and blows on the heart.

Fog rises from leaves.
Someone in an apron runs accross the porch.

The whip bursts.
The sun falls.

Are you here?
I don't know, Unnamed, I don't know.
Look at me.
Look at me.
When you like.
When I die.
When it shines.
When my body is extinguished.
When I breathe.
When I go.
I didn't write like this yet.
I don't know what will happen.
I see stars.
Does it spin round?
I don't know what spins round.
Can one hear?
I'm out of the cup.
I eat bran.
You found the cap.
I put on pyjamas.
Everything goes into me.
I glued myself.
I write slowly.
You are, what I see.

When I'll breathe, I'll die.
The reward is terrible.
I have everything.
There're lumberjacks.
The hour came.
There're apricots.
I hear touches.
There's a lock.
They said.
They danced.
Give me your cap.
I breathed.
I fell asleep.
You were fast.
I was late.
I have heard.